CELTIC CIRCLES

BONNIE RIDEOUT
SCOTTISH FIDDLE

A MUSICAL PICTURE THROUGH TIME
JOINING CYCLES OF HEAVEN AND EARTH
WITH CYCLES OF EVERYDAY LIFE

A recording of the music in this book is now available. The publisher strongly recommends the use of this recording along with the text to insure accuracy of interpretation and ease in learning.

This book is dedicated to

MARTHA FROSETH
and
BOB PHILLIPS

for their spirit and encouragement teaching hundreds
of young musicians in the
public schools of Saline, Michigan.

Table of Contents

THE MUSIC

Acknowledgments

I would like to express many thanks to the musicians involved in the initial recording, "Celtic Circles" (Al Petteway, Eric Rigler, Charlie Wilkie, Maggie Sansone, Charlie Pilzer, Myron Bretholz, Sue Richards, and Carolyn Surrick). Their musical contributions greatly enhanced the selections printed in this book.

To Connie McKenna and Myron Bretholz for helping with the text.

To my mother, Betty Rideout, for writing the chords, and my father, Doug Rideout, for his additional support.

A special debt of gratitude to my husband, Jesus Medrano, for his endless patience with me and our three children.

CELTIC CIRCLES cover design by Peg Udall
Cover Photograph by Gerald Hawkins c 1982
Musician photograph by Jesus Medrano
Originally engineered by
Bill McElroy at Bias Studios, Springfield, VA
With additional assistance from
Jim Robeson and Heidi Gerber
Produced by Charlie Pilzer

CELTIC CIRCLES is dedicated to the memory of two friends and mentors who provided both personal and musical inspiration:

RON GONNELLA (1930-1994) and **RUSSELL WOOLLEN (1923-1994)**

HERE'S WHAT THEY'RE SAYING

"Celtic Circles" underscores what different sounds a Celtic day makes: ...Time passes swiftly here, but also soulfully, elegantly and intelligently, as Rideout's instrumental flair and emotional sensitivity (on both fiddle and viola) are consistently enhanced by her impressive scholarship."
—WASHINGTON POST

"Celtic Circles" carries a sense of passion, pensive longing, vital beauty and poigancy...Fiddle champion, Bonnie Rideout, displays her deft and sensitive skill."
—HEARTSONG REVIEW

"Celtic Circles"..A Scots fiddle album with a difference...its reels, jigs and marches are fresh and vital while its slow airs have a forlorn beauty...a treasure trove of undiscovered gems."
—ROCK 'N REEL (U.K.)

Biography

While searching for hidden Christmas presents in her mother's closet, Bonnie Rideout came upon a dusty, black, oblong-shaped cardboard box. The old violin resting inside became her first love. That was in 1970; Bonnie was eight years old.

Bonnie Elisabeth Rideout grew up on a "retired" farm in Michigan, but spent much of her childhood on an island in Casco Bay, Maine, where she studied in a one-room school house. "It was on Cliff Island where I learned the importance of playing by ear," she recalls. "Our teacher, Miss Von Tiling, would gather all nine pupils and march us down the road playing the state song of Maine. My brother led the parade playing his trumpet, followed by the others on cymbals and drums, with me in the rear playing my violin. There was no possibility of reading music."

Bonnie's training in the oral tradition continued in Michigan, she says. "I scratched away on my fiddle while mom played the piano and dad tooted on his ocarinas. We played everything from 'The Moxie Song' to 'I Belong to Glasgow'. Playing by ear was so natural. It was at the heart of my most joyful music-making."

Bonnie received her formal violin training in Michigan. She played in public school orchestras and youth symphonies and took private violin instruction at the University of Michigan. She began college as a viola major but returned to the violin to finish her music and fine arts degrees in 1985. "I'm indebted to the teachers who taught me the discipline of reading music and playing the works of the 'masters,'" she says. "But the more I played 'serious' music, the more I missed my fiddling." At the time she knew nothing of the folk world but had happy memories of music making at home. It was the playing of renowned Scottish fiddler Dr. John Turner that opened a new world to her.

During the past ten years Bonnie has immersed herself in the music of her ancestral Scotland. She has lived and worked in Scotland: fusing the traditions of her Scottish-American upbringing with those of the old country. She played with numerous strathspey and reel societies in Scotland and learned the different styles of fiddling from such greats as Ron Gonnella, Bill Hardie, and Angus Cameron. "Perhaps I was most influenced by an Aberdeenshire farmer, Jim Falconer (and his wife Katherine), who kindly took me into his home," she recalls. "Jim played the fiddle and spent many evenings by the fire coaching me and tearing away my 'classical' edges."

Her labors have made her a three-time U.S. National Scottish fiddle champion and brought her prizes in many fiddle competitions in North America and Europe. She frequently performs, adjudicates, and teaches on both sides of the Atlantic. She records for the Maggie's Music label and, in addition to her solo career, Bonnie is a mother of three. She resides with her husband in Alexandria, Virginia.

CM

Photo by Irene Young

Introduction

Traditional music is best transmitted orally. With this in mind, I ask the reader of this book to understand that the black dots on the following pages represent only half the story. There isn't one "proper" way of playing this music nor writing it down. The selections have been drawn from my recording, "Celtic Circles." It would be impossible for me to write down all my bowings and every grace note, and yet these are important aspects of the music. Thus, the recording provides an invaluable guide to one particular interpretation of these tunes. The chords accompanying the music are not representative of what each musician recorded, but rather are simplified versions designed to furnish guitarists with a general idea of the chordal structure. I encourage any serious student of Scottish fiddle music to listen to as many different traditional recordings as possible, not to mention making the journey to Scotland. In addition, it is important to keep your ears and mind open to the music performed on instruments such as pipes, harp, whistle, flute, and most importantly the human voice.

About the Music

Circles and spirals have been used as symbols of life in civilizations from the Stone Age to modern times. Whether depicting the observance of the cycles of heaven and earth or the continuum of everyday life (day to night, birth to death), the circular theme is a vivid and recurring one in my mind.

"Celtic Circles" began as a visual project. Before becoming a full time mother and musician, I worked as an illustrator. In choosing musical selections that go well together, I think more in terms of color schemes and imaginary scenes which I visualize when learning a new tune. The cycle of the day became the initial theme. Next came a collage of images. "Dawn" brought the rising sun, men marching off to battle, peasants going to the fields, fishermen to the sea, a child awakening its mother, and so forth. During "Noonday", I followed the initial scenes into the next progression: a dance of two lovers in the sun, a battle cry and combat, children playing in the fields, rain falling on the fishermen, etc.. From these images -- continuing throughout the day until night -- I began choosing music that seemed to fit. As a result, the recording was sequenced from the start. Even in the studio we would refer to the music as "the drunken brawl set" or the "fallen warrior piece" instead of by their proper titles. In order to complete the cycle, the music on the closing track is intended to be followed by the first track again (so similar are the moods, keys, and instrumentation of both tracks).

The same holds true when reading through the music in this collection. It is my hope that while playing this music you will join the circle that inspired this work.

North Highland Tunes

No. 1

Traditional
Arranged by Bonnie Rideout

North Highland Tunes

No. 2

Traditional
Arranged by Bonnie Rideout

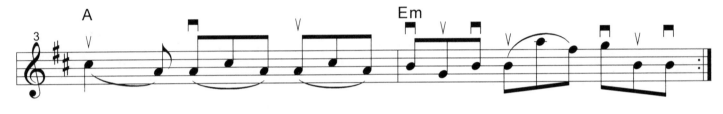

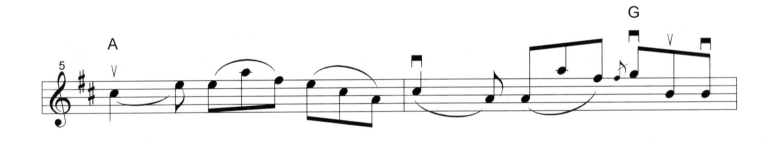

North Highland Tunes

Traditional
Arrangement by Bonnie Rideout

No. 3

Mary Do It Again

Traditional
Arranged by Bonnie Rideout

14

Cross Roads

Traditional
Arrangement by Bonnie Rideout

Jig In A

Traditional
Arranged by Bonnie Rideout

❋ Drone Omitting 3rd Throughout

Lament on the Death of Sor Blanca Maria

Bonnie Rideout ©

MacDonald Lord of the Isles

Traditional
Arranged by Bonnie Rideout

MacDonald Lord of the Isles - Continued

Romance

Ghillie Callum

Traditional
Arranged by Bonnie Rideout

Highlandman's Rant

Traditional

Arranged by Bonnie Rideout

Ryan's Rant

Traditional

Arranged by Bonnie Rideout

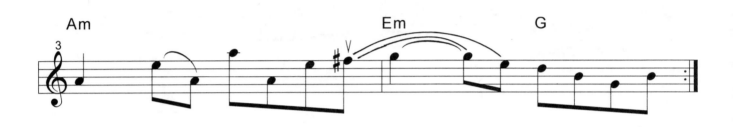

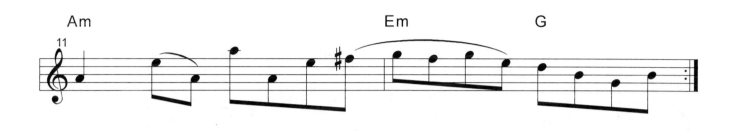

An Air to Which Ossian is Recited

Traditional
Arranged by Bonnie Rideout

The Boat Hoisted The Sails

Traditional

Arranged by Bonnie Rideout

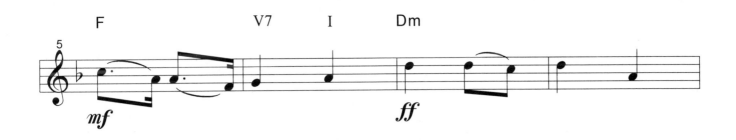

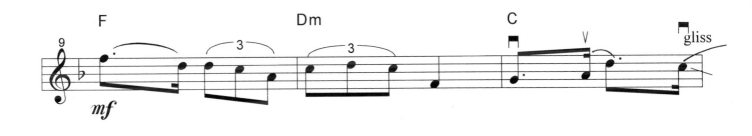

25

My Love Is Gone To Sea

Traditional
Arranged by Bonnie Rideout

26

Bog an Lochan

Traditional
Arranged by Bonnie Rideout

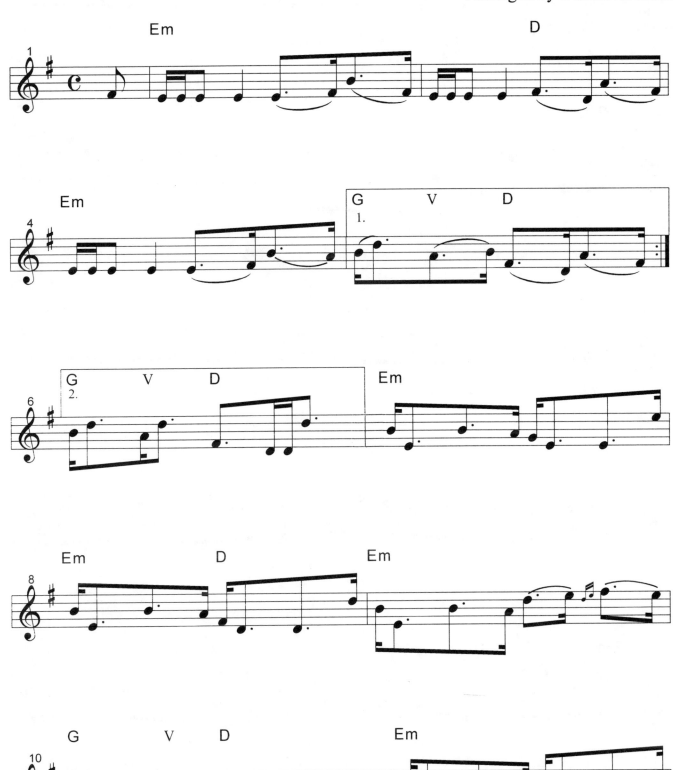

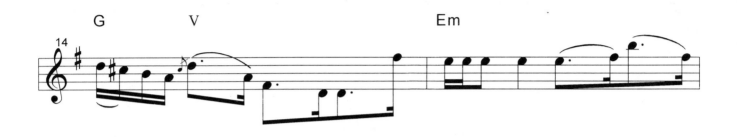

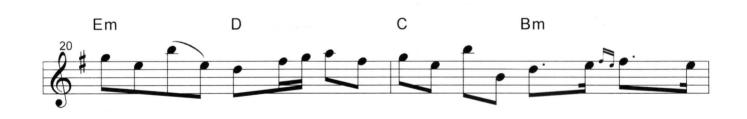

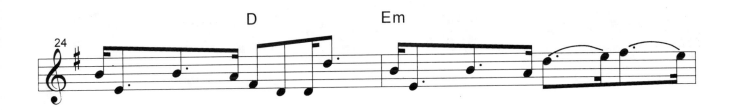

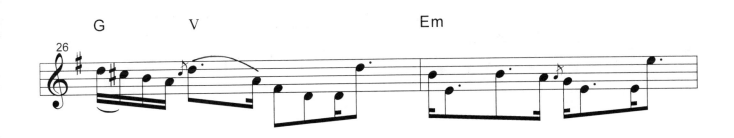

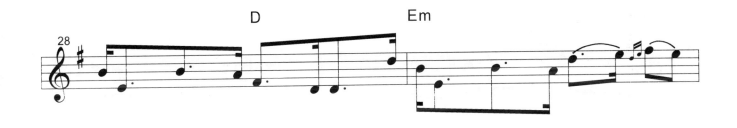

Drowsy Maggie

Traditional
Arranged Bonnie Rideout

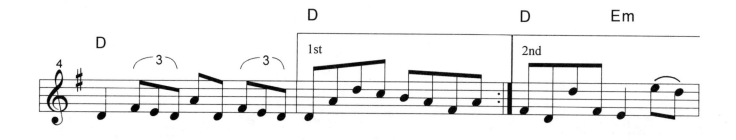

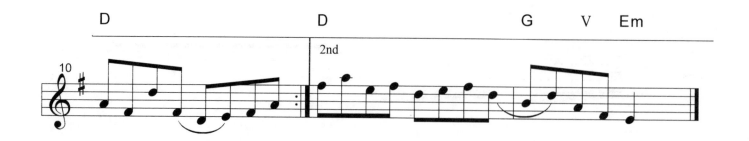

Sleeping Maggie

Traditional
Arranged by Bonnie Rideout

A Mother's Lament on the Death of Her Child

Traditional
Arranged by Bonnie Rideout

Violin I

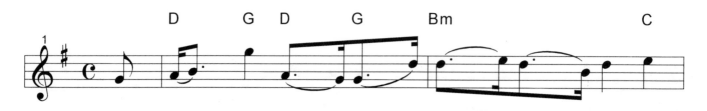

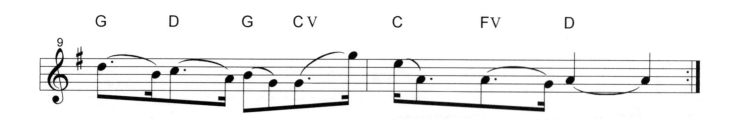

A Mother's Lament on the Death of Her Child

Violin II

A Dream

Traditional
Arranged by Bonnie Rideout

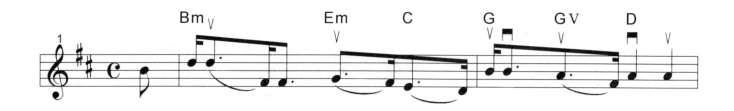

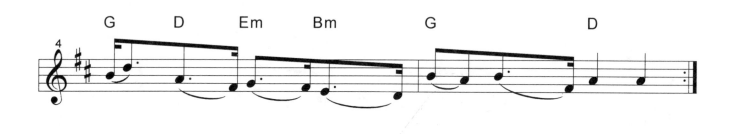

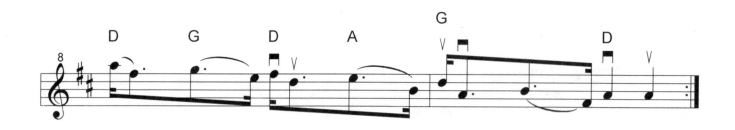

34

The Flo'ers O' the Forest

Traditional
Arranged by Bonnie Rideout

Yell Yell

Traditional
Arranged by Bonnie Rideout

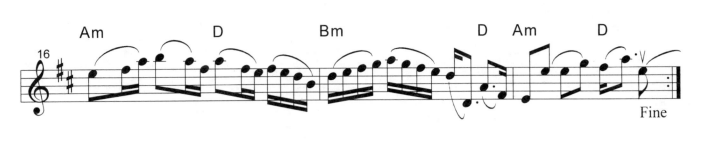
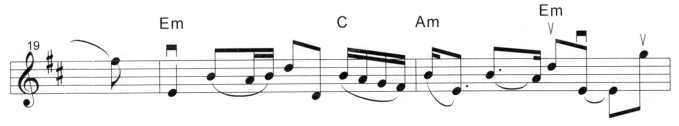
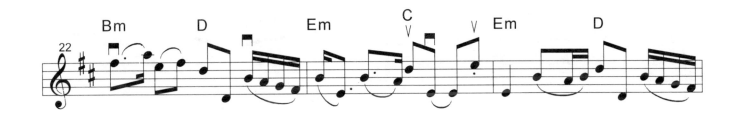
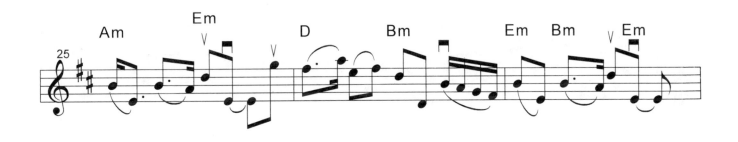

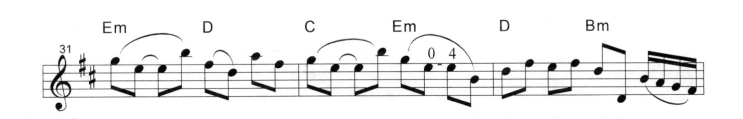

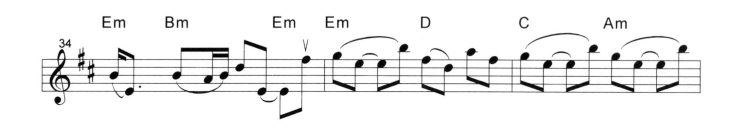

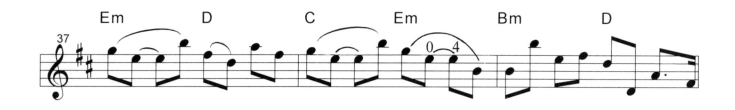

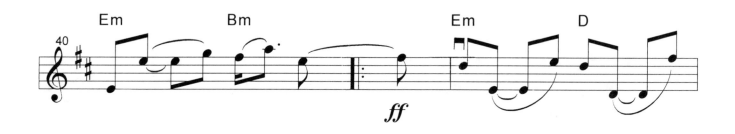

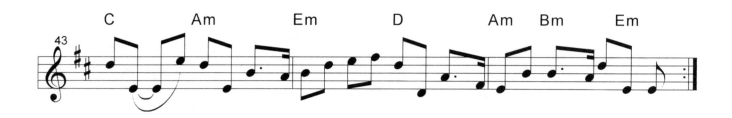

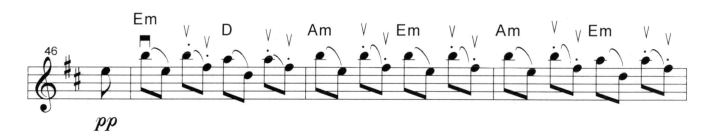

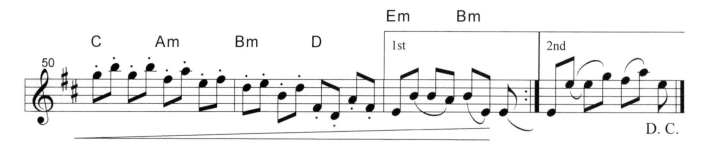

Prince Charlie's Farewell to Scotland

Traditional
Arranged by Bonnie Rideout

Fine

42

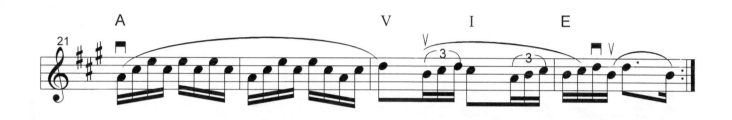

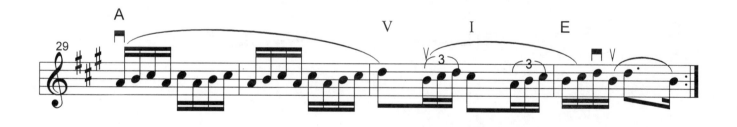

Winyadepla

Traditional
Arranged by Bonnie Rideout

44

Notes on the Music

THREE NORTH HIGHLAND TUNES (p. 11)
These three untitled tunes are numbered two, three, and four in the Patrick MacDonald Collection (1784). I have drawn more music for my recordings from this particular manuscript than from any other source of printed material.

MARY DO IT AGAIN / CROSS ROADS / JIG IN A (p. 14)
Three jigs, all of which appeared in Book XI of James Kerr's fourth Collection of Merry Melodies (from approx. 1875). Kerr was a Glasgow publisher and these particular tunes, although popular in Scotland at least since the nineteenth century, originated in Ireland. The second jig is similar to the Irish jig "Paudeen O'Rafferty" and the third jig is similar to the Irish jig "The Fair-Haired Boy". Because of its lyrical quality, I enjoy playing the first jig of the set as a slow air before moving into quick time.

LAMENT ON THE DEATH OF SOR BLANCA MARIA (p. 17)
A lament I wrote — most likely under the influence of Rev. Patrick MacDonald — in memory of my husband's aunt, Sor Blanca Maria. Maria Pastora Cruz was born in LaIquala, Honduras, C.A., in 1938. She served as a nun for the School Sisters of Notre Dame until her untimely death of cancer in 1993.

MAC DHOMHNUILL MOR NAN EILEAN (MacDonald Lord of the Isles) /
FONN UIRSGEUL NO DAN (Romance or Song Air) (p. 18)
The Fraser Collection (1st edition, 1816) is the source for this beautiful air. The text which accompanies this tune indicates that it is "possibly the most ancient air" in the collection. Although the timing in which I recorded this is different than the written page, I could not resist the shy tentativeness in the beginning lines: as two lovers begin to dance their first waltz, soon to get lost in their dance, only to become awkwardly self-conscious in the closing lines.

GHILLIE CALLUM / HIGHLANDMAN'S RANT / RYAN'S RANT (p. 20)
Another set of reels from the Kerr collection. While living on the Isle of Skye, I was told the tale of one Gillie Callum from Raasay, who drowned after his boat was sunk. That version of the story, which dates from around the end of the 17th century, had his wicked stepmother performing evil incantations in order to bring about the disaster. I do not know whether this is the same hapless victim for whom the first tune is named, but I think of him when I perform it.

FONN GNATHAICHTE DO BHRIATHRAIBH OISEIN
(An Air to which Ossian is Recited) (p. 24)
Although it was thought to be derived from ancient times, the epic poem called "Ossian" was actually written by 18th century poet James MacPherson. In its time, the poem's popularity was such that both Brahms and Schubert wrote music to its lyrics; I suspect that this particular tune predates the poem by many years. The sound of the small pipes and the fiddle is perfect for this tune, although I hope to hear it sung some day between tenor and alto voices.

THOG AM BATA NA SIUIL (The Boat Hoisted the Sails) /
CHAIDH MO LEANNAN NULL THAT SAL (My Love Is Gone to Sea) (p. 25)
A waulking song and a slow air which is often played in quicker tempo for dances. The first tune would have been sung while shrinking tweed, a process known as "waulking." After removing the cloth from the loom, the ends of the fabric were sewn together to form a circle and the resulting piece was soaked in warm urine in order to soften the cloth and set the color of the dye. Then, two rows of women seated facing each other at a long board or table would knead the cloth and pass it clockwise around the table until the fabric had sufficiently shrunk. The first tune can be played as a round. It is a nice coincidence that these two pieces work well together not only musically but thematically as well.

BOG AN LOCHAN (The Water Ouzel) / **DROWSY MAGGIE / SLEEPING MAGGIE** (p. 27)
Charlie Wilkie, a fine guitarist from Detroit whom I have played with for over 15 years, introduced me to "Bog an Lochan." It was the first strathspey I learned with guitar (having always played with my mother accompanying me on piano). These tunes are popular in sessions from the U.S. and Cape Breton to Ireland and Scotland: often played at breathtaking speeds.

A MOTHER'S LAMENT ON THE DEATH OF HER CHILD / AISLING (A Dream) (p. 32)
These two pieces (#'s 175 and 169) in the Patrick MacDonald Collection seem to fit together beautifully, although each stands perfectly on its own. I once used the first tune in a competition set with my own improvised variations and double stops. Although I have written a basic harmony part, the more I perform them, the more I understand that both tunes deserve to be played simply and without much ornamentation (including vibrato!).

FLO'ERS O' THE FOREST (p. 36)
This lament commemorates the catastrophic Battle of Flodden Field which was fought on English soil in 1513. The battle saw the slaying of King James IV and many of the brightest stars of the Scottish nobility. With their departure, the Scottish renaissance which James inspired was brutally stamped out. Arrangements of this music are commonly performed at funerals and memorial events all over the globe.

YELL YELL (p. 38)
From *The Beauties of Niel Gow Collection* (part 1, 1784). This tune is described in the text as "very old". I am not sure whether the title refers to the excessive use of the vocal chords or the Isle of Yell. Once, after becoming separated from my family in a large international airport, I took out my fiddle and began playing this tune very loudly. They found me instantly.

PRINCE CHARLIE'S FAREWELL TO SCOTLAND / WINYADEPLA (p. 42)
Following the calamitous defeat at Culloden on April 16, 1745, the Jacobite efforts to give the throne back to the Stuarts were smashed. After the battle, Prince Charles Edward Stuart spent five perilous months in hiding. Despite a bounty of £30,000 being placed on his head, he was never betrayed by his Scottish brethren. Finally, in September of that year, he was able to obtain passage on a frigate bound for France and permanent exile. This farewell lament brings one almost on board that ship with the Prince as he is sailing away. "Winyadepla" is taken from *Da Mirrie Dances,* a collection of Shetland fiddle tunes edited by Tom Anderson and Tom Georgeson. The tune's title refers to a loch near the Fir Vaa watermill. According to the notes in the collection, in 1803 a man named Gibbie Laurenson heard the tune coming from a troop of peerie folk. When the tuned ended, he observed the trows rowing away in a little boat. The two tunes seem to blend together nicely, with the feel of the sea. On the *Celtic Circles* recording, I overlapped the two slightly and added a simple harmony before returning to the B section of the original tune and ending softly with the repeated sixteenth note turns.

 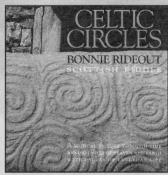